Personal Notes:

WELCOME WORDS FROM JF BROU AND IVAYLO

Dear Men,

Hi, I'm JF, Jean-Francois from Montreal, Canada. I started my self-development journey 12 years ago like most men, reading *The Game* by Neil Strauss and exploring the Pick Up Artist community. This book led me from one thing to another until I stumbled on *The 4-Hour Work Week* by Tim Ferriss.

Ever since reading that book, I've dreamed and acted on creating a life of traveling the world, working remotely, having immersive experiences and pushing myself out of my comfort zone. The road was not easy. but led me to incredible discovery, wisdom, meeting incredible people and having life-changing experiences.

Hi! I am Ivaylo, originally from Bulgaria and currently living in Medellin, Colombia. I began my spiritual journey 7 years ago after my mother passed away. I started with mindfulness meditation and slowly but surely got to know a lot of spiritual literature, gong baths, breathwork, inner child work, and plant medicine. In my search for my masculine identity, as well as in the process of healing my relationship with my own father, I became very passionate about men's work and helping other men reclaim their power and reconnect with their masculinity.

After leaving my corporate job in London in 2018, I came to Medellin where I co-founded People Like Us, a spiritual community where we come together with the intention of taking care of mind, body, and spirit; as well as taking care and supporting each other along the way. I facilitate Wim Hof Method practices (working towards becoming a certified instructor), Breathwork and Cacao Ceremonies, and Men's group work. With interests in various spiritual paths, I'm always looking to expand my consciousness and operate from a place of abundance.

We connected in another workshop and we kept in contact. Slowly we shared insights on our growth and became friends. We started to join experiences together, one of which was a private men's circle. From there, a random conversation happened about the idea of doing a workshop for men only. We got so excited that we jumped on the idea and launched our first men's workshop the next day.

THE STORY BEHIND WHY WE CREATED THIS WORKBOOK

We started this workbook out of offering our first workshop for men only. A bold offering since 70% of workshop attendees are women, but we had this big inner need to do it for 2 reasons. One, for ourselves, to deeply explore and take action on this superior look into men's insights. From struggling with our love relationship to wanting to be a more grounded, fulfilled and attractive man we realized this content was the key. Second, to connect deeply with other like-minded men bringing authentic support and community leading to blissful opportunities and connections.

WHAT DOES IT MEAN TO BECOME A SUPERIOR MAN?

Being a superior man means to be a never-ending deep student of life, but more precisely mastering the men's psyche knowledge and having a full understanding of how to connect with their feminine energy. Also, it means to be an example of reaching your highest potential, mentor, support, inspire others and take care of your community.

Being a superior man also means being fully responsible for yourself while facing life challenges with courage and optimism. Lastly, the ultimate purpose of a superior man is to break their heart wall to live every minute of their life with the open heart chakra, the core center of love and compassion.

Step by step we are bringing you on this journey through this workbook.

ARE YOU READY?
LET'S GET DOWN TO BUSINESS.

CHAPTER 1:

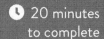
Boy vs. Man Psychology

The disappearance of male initiation rituals at various stages in life prevents modern men from growing up in certain ways, leaving them much poorer in spirit and mind.

In addition, the many cases of absent fathers, be it physically or emotionally, and the wide-spread demonization of masculinity, labeling it inherently abusive, negative and *toxic* contributes to modern men's inability to transcend the early developmental stages and fully embrace the full potential of the mature masculine energies. The results of these developments are evidenced by the precarious state of mental health for men, suicide rates, addiction, and depression likelihood, as well as unwillingness to ask for help.

Many men are grown up based on their age but are stuck in an immature stage of their development, we call it boy psychology and below we contrast it with man psychology.

BOY	MAN
Runs away from pain	Moves towards pleasure
Seeks external validation	Self-assured—focused on action, not approval
Dominates others	Nurtures others
Intimidated by others' wins	Inspired by others' wins
Scared of Failure	Actively pushes to failure
Puts others down	Lifts others up
Hides fear and insecurities	Embraces fear and works through insecurities
Doesn't follow through	Honors promises
Lives in scarcity	Lives in abundance
Driven by Ego	Driven by Higher Self

In summary, grown-up men acting like boys are at the root of society's problems because no one showed them how to step into their mature masculine power. It is our view that men nowadays are in need of more, not less, masculine energy, but of the mature type.

Here's questions allowing you to introspect on man models in your life:

Who has been a male role model for you in your life? What have you learned from them about being a man?

Name 1–3 younger men who could benefit from your mentorship / positive support:

What exactly could you do to help them move into a more mature stage of masculinity?

CHAPTER 2:

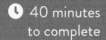
The Masculine Archetypes

What are archetypes you might ask? In the book "*King, Warrior, Magician, Lover: Rediscovering the Archetypes of the Mature Masculine*," Jungian psychologist Robert Moore and mythologist Douglas Gillette propose that masculinity is made up of four archetypal male energies which serve different purposes.

All men from all generations, all walks for life, and all geographic regions are born with these archetypal energies. The authors argue that, in order to become a complete man, one must work to develop all four archetypes. The result of striving to become complete is a feeling of manly confidence and purpose.

When a man is not in a conscious relationship with an archetype, he is automatically ruled by its bipolar shadow, often switching back and forth between the active and passive poles, completely at the mercy of events. We slide into the active shadow when there is inflation, or too much, of archetypal energy and the passive shadow when we feel a deflation, or too little, of said energy.

In this chapter, we offer information on the mature and shadow aspects of each archetype, as well as ways to connect fully with each of these energies.

2.1. THE KING

MATURE ASPECT

The King is the source of order and blessing in the kingdom (our life). In the kingdom of the wise and just king, laughter rings through the lands, life is abundant, and we approach it with excitement and creative life force.

In the psyche of the man, the King archetype is the central archetype, around which the rest of the psyche is organized. It helps us create our world, life vision, be self-assured and adapt to any situation life throws at us. If the King's energy in us is weak, our psyche falls in disarray, and chaos threatens our lands.

The man who is constantly overwhelmed by life—who can't seem to find harmony or order—must develop the King's energy, often in conjunction with Warrior energy to protect his borders.

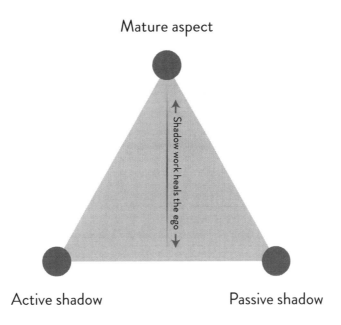

Active Shadow—The Tyrant
- Power is fragile—seeks to destroy all new life—the inner critic
- Ego inflation—seeks power and domination in order to cover up his enormous sense of insecurity
- Degrades others
- Sensitive to criticism and responds with rage
- Feeling fear and vulnerability

Passive Shadow—The Weakling
- Projects King energy onto others
- Not taking responsibility for one's life
- Helpless and Hopeless
- Overwhelmed
- Paranoid
- Fear of betrayal will inevitably cause him to switch over to the Tyrant to control others

How do you connect with this archetype day-to-day and give an example(s) of situation(s) where you have experienced operating from one or two of the shadow poles.

....

....

....

....

....

What could you do to connect better with the positive aspect of this energy?

....

....

....

....

....

Here's how to access the King:

- Take full responsibility for everything in your life
- Create a vision board
- Set goals
- Live with more integrity than you currently do
- Meditate on what is important to you in life
- Live by your own internal code
- Start/join a men's group
- Express encouragement and praise for others

From the knowledge above and experience, what are the things you will do to access the King?

....

....

....

....

....

2.2. THE MAGICIAN

MATURE ASPECT

The Magician is the thinker and all aspects of life where learning is required to come under the energy of the Magician. He is the wise man, the sage, the knower of secrets. He sees and navigates the inner worlds; he understands the dynamics and energy flows of the outer. He is a master of technology, engineering, mathematics, mysticism, and logic.

The Magician has the capacity to detach from events—the chaos of the world—and draw on essential truths and resources deep within him. He thinks clearly in times of crisis and enables us to take a broader view of things.

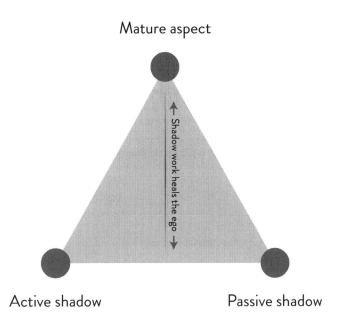

Mature aspect

Shadow work heals the ego

Active shadow

Passive shadow

Active Shadow—The Detached Manipulator
*   Works to undermine others—to make them inferior to himself
*   Feels better than others for the knowledge he possesses
*   Not sharing knowledge as it feels as giving away power
*   Use knowledge to attack and control others

Passive Shadow—The Denying Innocent One
*   Wants recognition, but not willing to do the work to earn it
*   Fears others' talents and their growth as they would outshine him
*   Lazy
*   Envious

How do you connect with this archetype day-to-day and give an example(s) of situation(s) where you have experienced operating from one or two of the shadow poles.

....

....

....

....

What could you do to connect better with the positive aspect of this energy?

....

....

....

....

Here's how to access the Magician:

- Dedicate yourself to a craft or primary mission in your life
- Find a mentor and listen well
- Create more
- Understand that certain lessons must come once you have truly earned them
- Study anything
- Study the KWML archetypes
- Take up spirituality in order to penetrate the mysteries of the Universe
- Teach something

From the knowledge above and experience, what are the things you will do to access the Magician?

....

....

....

....

2.3. THE WARRIOR

MATURE ASPECT

The warrior is a powerhouse of energy, the source of which is a transpersonal commitment to a higher purpose. This is the energy that brings us discipline, consistency, commitment, will power, and the strength to keep going forward despite difficulties we might encounter.

The warrior destroys what is negative and harmful. The warrior is a doer, not a thinker. He is a master tactician, knowing at all times his limitations, and finds creative ways around them. He is a little «unhuman», always chasing his next big goal, always putting emphasis on his mission as opposed to his relationships.

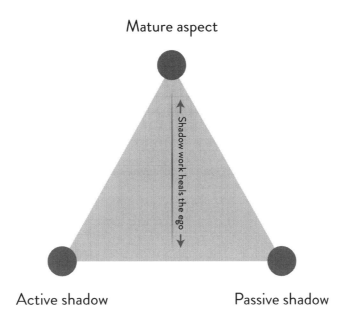

Mature aspect

Shadow work heals the ego

Active shadow   Passive shadow

Active Shadow—The Sadist
- Hates weakness and vulnerability
- Tormenting others who remind him of his passive shadow (Masochist)
- Cruel
- Self-destructive—brings anxiety, burnout
- Represses emotions
- Uncontrolled aggression, violence

Passive Shadow—The Masochist
- Projects Warrior energy onto others
- Experiences himself as impotent and vulnerable
- Cannot stand up for himself
- Tolerates abuse until one day he snaps and shift to the Sadist Pole

How do you connect with this archetype day-to-day and give an example(s) of situation(s) where you have experienced operating from one or two of the shadow poles.

....

....

....

....

....

What could you do to connect better with the positive aspect of this energy?

....

....

....

....

....

Here's how to access the Warrior:
- Challenge yourself
- Take up martial arts
- Exercise
- Work on your sense of discipline
- Engage in a confrontation you have postponed
- Always tell the truth
- Maintain perfect integrity
- Work on maintaining good boundaries

From the knowledge above and experience, what are the things you will do to access the Warrior?

....

....

....

....

....

2.4. THE LOVER

MATURE ASPECT

The lover is finely attuned to the realm of the senses and worships beauty. He is a musician, poet and artist, and a lover of all things, both inner and outer. He wants to always stay connected, and does not recognize boundaries. He wants to experience the world as one ongoing big orgasm of hearts uniting as One. He is the mystic who feels everything as himself, and the source of all intuition.

Through his feeling capacity, he is finely attuned to people's energy, capable of reading them like an open book. Whereas the other archetypes bring structure to the male psyche, the lover has no structure but fills said structure with aliveness, beauty and flavour.

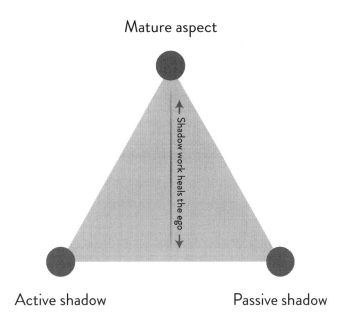

Active Shadow—The Addicted Lover
- Constant fulfilment of sensual desires
- Unstable internal structures—lacking direction
- Not knowing what he truly looks for—all the while seeking endless pleasure
- Uses substances to manage emotions

Passive Shadow—The Impotent Lover
- Chronically Depressed
- Feels cut off from himself and others, withdrawn
- Has lost his desire for life, low energy
- Sexually inactive
- His feelings of being stuck and unsatisfied may push him towards to the Addicted Lover

How do you connect with this archetype day-to-day and give an example(s) of situation(s) where you have experienced operating from one or two of the shadow poles.

How do you connect with this archetype day-to-day and give an example(s) of situation(s) where you have
experienced operating from one or two of the shadow poles.

What could you do to connect better with the positive aspect of this energy?

Here's how to access the Lover:
- Slow down and see the beauty in simple things, instead of consuming more
- Express your appreciation of beauty
- Spend time in nature
- Turn sex into your art
- Listen to music that moves you (yes, move with it) and make really enjoying it a practice of presence
- Take up dance lessons
- Start playing an instrument
- Sing

From the knowledge above and experience, what are the things you will do to access the Lover?

Superior Man Mindsets, Beliefs and Habits

A superior man has certain traits and behaviors to himself that we can reverse engineer, meaning we can deconstruct his persona and take action on the road map step by step.

3.1. SUPERIOR MAN MINDSETS

🕐 5 minutes to complete

Mindsets are conscious attitudes a man needs to take to reach his next level. Here's a list that you should continue with your own insights:

- Self Love is my foundation
- Driven by purpose and freedom, purpose before relationships
- Mastering woman's needs and way of thinking
- Never change your mind to please a women = weakening your wisdom
- Self-fulfilled, self-mastery, self-exploration
- Eliminates excuses, consistent winner
- Calm, assertive, expand under stress
- Willing to listen and learn, student of life
- Seeks meaningful experiences, follow your intuition, have directions
- Retention (no ejaculation), Sublimation, keep your life force
- Connect often with the feminine energy: beer, nature, radiant women

List other mindsets of a superior man you would like to keep in mind:

....

....

....

....

....

3.2. SUPERIOR MAN BELIEFS

🕐 5 minutes to complete

Beliefs are subconscious patterns a man develops from his parents or environment as a child. We need to bring awareness to those self-limiting beliefs and change them with repetitive affirmations and actions. Here's a list you should continue with your own insights:

- I am abundant
- I am in charge
- I am attractive
- I am enough
- I am loved
- I am strong & unstoppable
- I am confident and powerful
- I am ambitious and purposeful
- I am loving and caring
- I am peace, understanding, forgiving, compassionate
- I am a superior man

List other beliefs of a superior man you would like to keep in mind:

....

....

....

....

....

....

....

....

....

....

....

....

3.3. SUPERIOR MAN HABITS

🕐 5 minutes to complete

Habits are conscious actions a man needs to take consistently every day to change his self-limiting beliefs and reach his higher self. We build habit with the Kaizen principle, setting the least minimum goal to reach consistently every day for 66 days to turn it into a lifestyle. Here's a list you should continue with your own insights:

- Meditation, Sports, Study, Discipline,
- Keep your heart chakra open when it hurts
- Regular reviews of goals
- Accept criticism
- Weekly activity to recenter in his masculine energy, grounding
- Present, mindful, active listener
- Inspire, support, mentor, nurture
- Retain ejaculation and sublimate into creative energy
- Breathe from the belly
- Take charge and direction for managing all life dimensions

List other habits of a superior man you would like to keep in mind:

....

....

....

....

....

....

....

....

....

....

....

3.4. VALUES & VIRTUES

🕐 10 minutes to complete

Habits need to match your values, otherwise it will be too hard to keep consistent actions on your habits. Here's a list you should continue with your own insights:
- Loyalty
- Commitment
- Open-mindedness
- Consistency
- Honesty
- Creativity
- Compassion
- Spirit of adventure
- Optimism
- Respect

List your top 10 values you live or would like to live by and then circle your top 3:

....

....

....

....

....

List virtues for your top 3 values:

Virtues are behaviors that make you act on those values daily/weekly even if you are exhausted or have no time that day/week.

1 ....

2 ....

3 ....

Superior Man Purpose & Freedom

Masculine energy is driven by Purpose and Freedom compared to Feminine energy is driven by Love and Family. A superior man is living deeply in his purpose making it the most important thing in his life.

If it's not the case his women will lose attraction toward him and even over time he will lose his life force becoming lazy and comfortable directing his attention toward things giving him momentarily purpose like being a team sport fan, playing a video game, challenging himself physically without pursuing the best in that discipline.

So here's an amazing exercise below to explore your current purpose that will lead you to the next one. They are life cycles like an onion layer, you're peeling purpose after purpose till your main core purpose is using your gift to help the universe with an open heart chakra.

IKIGAI

A Japanese concept meaning 'a reason for being'

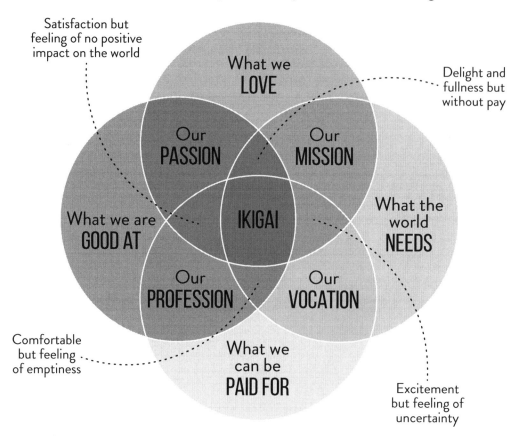

4.1. IKIGAI = A REASON FOR BEING

What do you LOVE? (in your personal and professional life, the contrary of what you hate)

....

....

....

....

....

What are you GOOD AT? (that you might like or not like to do)

....

....

....

....

....

What does the WORLD NEED? (from your own perspective & vision of the world)

....

....

....

....

....

What can I get PAID FOR? (the skills you bring on the table to grow your organization)

....

....

....

....

....

4.2. QUADRANT OF SUCCESS

What do you LOVE, plus are good at? (PASSION)

....
....
....
....

What don't you LOVE, plus are good at? (PAYING YOUR BILLS)

....
....
....
....

What do you LOVE, but you are not good at yet? (POTENTIAL) (learn more, not yet an expert)

....
....
....
....

What don't you LOVE, plus are not good at? (DAILY TASKS)

....
....
....
....

* We spend most of our lives on #3 and #4
** #1 & #2 requires deep investment and learning. You need to go all-in on those.

4.3. FIND YOUR WHY

https://courses.startwithwhy.com/

The reasons you will NEVER give up. (Family, purpose, past suffering, life situation, etc.)

What is the impact on my life if no change happens in the next 12 months. (family, relationships, work, health, etc.)

How will I show up differently to achieve success?

4.4. STATE YOUR PURPOSE IN ONE SENTENCE

Reason to wake up and grow, serve people/world, give back, inspire

....

....

....

....

....

....

4.5. WHAT AND WHEN IN YOUR WEEK IS TAKING OVER YOUR ATTENTION FOR MOMENTARILY PURPOSE AND FREEDOM?

The need for Freedom is the core of every man. You reach freedom by living on your own terms managing your time, money, energy and living with purpose. If not, a man will seek momentarily freedom with excessive ejaculation, winning at a recreational sport, having their sport fan team win a championship, zapping TV channels, etc. List the things you do to seek momentarily purpose and freedom.

....

....

....

....

....

....

....

....

....

....

How to Be a More Attractive Man

🕐 15 minutes
to complete

5.1. WHAT ARE YOUR MAN SELF-CARE ROUTINES AND WHAT ELSE COULD YOU DO TO BE A MORE ATTRACTIVE MAN?

Being confident with yourself starts with self-care routines. For example: Keeping your haircut and beard clean and stylish; reuniting your wardrobe style, doing sports, connecting with your inner child and other men, learning and working on yourself and connecting with man's divine power accessing the king, warrior, magician, and lover.

Right Now:

To add:

5.2. WHAT ARE YOUR SOFT SKILLS QUALITIES AND WHAT ELSE COULD YOU DO TO BE A MORE ATTRACTIVE MAN?

Soft skills are a combination of people skills, social skills, communication skills, character or personality traits, attitudes, career attributes, social intelligence, and emotional intelligence. For example public speaking, active listening, a small act of kindness, deep self-love, disrespect, and honesty.

Right Now:

....

....

....

....

....

To add:

....

....

....

....

....

Emotions and Man's Energy

Emotions are the subject that will free you from all your suffering. 93% of humans have a heart wall coming from trapped emotions lived in their first 7 years of their lives. The heart wall is a metaphor meaning your heart chakra opens and closes easily many times a day with your thoughts and reaction to life situations. Your heart chakra is the center core where all the energy of love comes in and out. A blocked heart chakra will lead you to act out of fear.

Your trapped emotions are relieved over and over again through your life each time a situation triggers them. The thing is, we naturally think is that specific situation that makes us react like that, but it is only a trigger to hit something that has been sleeping inside.

6.1. RELEASING TRAPPED EMOTIONS THROUGH MUSCLE TESTING WITH THE EMOTION CHART

Trapped emotions create balls of energy in specific organs of your body that, over the years, start ripping off the tissue of these organs. From Chinese Traditional Medicine (TCM), we have 5 core organs trapping 5 types of emotions which are not letting the Qi energy (the vital energy, energy of love) circulate properly through those organs. New theories think this is the cause of every cancer. Watch the documentary Heal on Netflix and E-motions on Gaia.

Dr. Bradley Nelson invented a legendary technique to find our trapped emotions and open the gates to relive them so we can release them for good. Using the muscle testing technique with the emotion code chart below, you access your subconscious mind to find 5-6 emotions trapped in a session of one hour. You then usually relive those emotions in the next 1 to 5 days. You then go back to doing session after session with a few weeks' intervals.

Watch these videos explaining the process:
Bradley Nelson Demonstrates Muscle Testing and Emotion Code
https://www.youtube.com/watch?v=yPrHryxxbc8

Emotion Code—Process of Releasing Trapped Emotion
https://www.youtube.com/watch?v=N7S66OSNDil&

Definition of emotions:
http://www.themarriagelibrary.com/EmotionCode/Definition-of-Emotions.pdf

	COLUMN A	COLUMN B
THE EMOTION CODE™ CHART		
Row 1 Heart or Small Intestine	Abandonment Betrayal Forlorn Lost Love Unreceived	Effort Unreceived Heartache Insecurity Overjoy Vulnerability
Row 2 Spleen or Stomach	Anxiety Despair Disgust Nervousness Worry	Failure Helplessness Hopelessness Lack of Control Low Self-Esteem
Row 3 Lung or Colon	Crying Discouragement Rejection Sadness Sorrow	Confusion Defensiveness Grief Self-Abuse Stubborness
Row 4 Liver or Gall Bladder	Anger Bitterness Guilt Hatred Resentment	Depression Frustration Indecisiveness Panic Taken for Granted
Row 5 Kidneys or Bladder	Blaming Dread Fear Horror Peeved	Conflict Creative Insecurity Terror Unsupported Wishy Washy
Row 6 Glands & Sexual Organs	Humiliation Jealousy Longing Lust Overwhelm	Pride Shame Shock Unworthy Worthless

I have a trapped emotion of .... from the age of ....

related with .... (person)

because of .... (situation).

I have a trapped emotion of .... from the age of ....

related with .... (person)

because of .... (situation).

I have a trapped emotion of .... from the age of ....

related with .... (person)

because of .... (situation).

I have a trapped emotion of .... from the age of ....

related with .... (person)

because of .... (situation).

I have a trapped emotion of .... from the age of ....

related with .... (person)

because of .... (situation).

6.2. EMOTIONAL SURRENDER

This moment is not a mistake. The Universe is asking you to look directly at it and be fully in it, even if it hurts for a few minutes. Surrender to this process and your work and joy happen more quickly. You will transform.

Here's the great news. You don't need to know how to do this, even though I will tell you. Your body knows exactly what to do. You will see that your body wants to do this. If you just can't let it do its work, you will move stuck energy.

Here is a simple version of the process. You can do this in the morning when you wake up or when you feel an uncomfortable emotion happening for you.

THE EMOTIONAL SURRENDER PROCESS
1. Sit somewhere quiet.
2. Set a timer for 15 minutes.
3. Start breathing a little faster than normal, but at a steady pace.
4. **Breathe with the belly.** Fill the belly with air as low in your body as you can. Breathe in and out from this spot purposely for the duration of this process. If you forget to do this, that's fine, just start again.
5. Feel the emotion or emotions happening for you. Let them come. For just a few minutes today, you are going to welcome your experience.
6. **As the emotion happens, find the** physical **sensations of it.** Where is it in the body? Does it feel hard or soft? Is it hot? Is it trembling? Is it tight? Do not try to analyze anything. You may have thoughts about the emotion or thoughts about what you should do to "fix" the situation. You can't fix it. Ignore these thoughts. You may have thoughts that say you should not or don't have to feel what you are feeling. Ignore these thoughts. Focus entirely on physical sensations.

Put your awareness into the physical sensations and find out what they are. You can even use your mind to describe them out loud.

7. Let them get stronger. Invite the physical sensations to come. This is your actual felt experience of the emotion and you can handle the physical sensations. They are actually much easier to handle than thoughts. You do not have to know what the emotion even is or why it is happening. Very often those insights will come automatically. You don't have to look for them. Just stay focused on the *physical* sensations and keep belly breathing.

8. **Now relax into these sensations and surrender to your body.** Don't try to change anything. Just surrender. Just put your awareness on the physical sensations and stop trying to resist anything. Let them happen fully. Let your body have control. Let it do whatever it wants. Stand, bend over, lie down, shake, hum, make noise, cry, laugh, scream (into a pillow), squirm on the floor, twist and turn, curl into a ball, shake your hands, stomp, punch (a pillow). All of this body activity is your cells naturally moving the old stuck energy and releasing. Let them do it.

9. **Keep your belly breathing. All the time.** Keep your belly breathing and focusing on the body sensations. Most likely they will come in waves. They will build up and it will seem hard to handle. Just keep relaxing into it and surrendering to the body. This is your body trying to heal. The wave will subside and you might feel relief or peace. And another wave might come. Or that particular disturbance might be done, forever.

10. **The timer will go off in 15 minutes and you are done.** That's it. No need to force yourself. 15 minutes is enough. You might find, however, once you learn how energy moves through you and once you encounter the peace and relief on the other side of your emotions, you might want to continue this process until the waves are complete. You might find it is actually easy to let these things happen. And then they are done, and the emotion is gone. You might find you actually enjoy it.

What is actually happening in this process? You are surrendering to what the Universe is asking you to look at. You are surrendering to the energy that needs to move through your body. When you give these hurts parts of your full awareness and acceptance you reconnect it with your love. You are welcoming it and embracing it, and letting it come through you, and this heals it! Emotional surrender lets healing happen. Your body knows what to do, we are just restricting it almost all the time. Give your body the gift of freedom, just for a few minutes today.

If you want to be a little more active with your mind in this process, you can consciously drop your defenses, open your heart, and you can literally invite the sensations, emotions, and energy through your heart.

*Reference: This exercise was taken from the newsletter of Coach David Papa. https://www.davidpapa.live/

Enlighten Sexuality

CHAPTER 7 :

🕐 25 minutes
to complete

7.1. A SUPERIOR MAN EJACULATES UP THE SPINE

Ever since our hormones changed as teenagers we practice and naturally ejaculate. What we don't realize is we throw away 300 billion sperm from our body on average for each ejaculation and it takes around 72 hours to rebuild that amount in our testicles. You might have realized that after ejaculation you just want to pass out or have low energy.

This is normal, you just lost your life force. The superior man doesn't ejaculate, if he does it's with a clear intention to be deliberate before the act. And don't worry, ejaculation does equal orgasm, and by ejaculating up the spine you'll build longer full-body orgasms.

But it takes patience and practice, you have a lifelong bad habit to change. Here's the step by step to master:

PRACTICE RETENTION

1. Each time you go pee, let it out, hold it for 15 seconds, let it out, hold it for 15 seconds. Like this, you are strengthening your urethral sphincter muscles.
2. From now on, when masturbating and when you are 90% ready to ejaculate, press on the million-dollar point between your testicles and your anus or contract your pelvic floor. This will block the ejaculatory vessel from your testicles to your urethral.
3. Every day, work on strengthening your whole pelvic floor muscles by sucking upward your anus, pelvic floor, and scrotum. This will strengthen your muscles and with time will enable you to control your ejaculation.

PRACTICE SUBLIMATION

4. Experience different breathwork techniques before your daily meditation practice. Examples: Holotropic breathwork, Fire breathwork, Wim Hof breathwork

5. While masturbating, start your sublimation practice. Breath into the nose all the way down your belly, after your belly is inflated, push it back in slowly exhaling while circulating your sacral chakra energy through up your spine, passing chakra by chakra all the way up to your crown chakra and then coming back in front to your third eye chakra.

6. Practice, practice, practice. Fail a lot. Combine retention with sublimation.

NON-EJACULATORY ORGASMS

7. When you reach the point of no return at around 95% just contract your pelvic floor combined with the breathwork. Yes it's hard to do both at the same time, but with practice, you'll get there. Your orgasms will be longer, 30-45 seconds instead of 10-15 seconds, more intense and will energize you instead of depleting you.

Take notes on your discoveries:

7.2. HOW TO PLEASE YOUR WOMEN SEXUALLY

The sex languages of women are touch and smell compared to men's being sight and sound. Before each main sexual act, prepare the room with the right settings: light, essence, sexual music, and a comfy blanket. Then start your preliminary using the tip of your fingers with the intention of creating electricity by slightly touching her neck, arms, chess, face and any other undressed parts. The longer and more teasing the preliminaries are, the harder your women will come.

Describe an experience where you satisfy your woman's primary sexual language of touch and smell:

7.3. SEX LIFE DATE IDEAS BOOSTING YOUR ROMANTIC RELATIONSHIP

Your women want you to take directions, control, be surprising and creative. Come up with detail oriented sex dates. For example:

1. Prepare a sexual game preliminary: cards, dice, trivia questions, etc.
2. Prepare the best sex playlist on her taste, set your room with candles, scents, decorations and offer her a full body super oily massage.
3. Change setting, for example going to a love motel where you paid for the extra service with the room decoration, bubble bath in the jacuzzi, and flowers everywhere

List 3 sex date ideas you will organize for your women:

Men vs. Women's Brain

8.1. MEN VS. WOMEN'S MAIN CHARACTERISTICS

We often forget that we, man and woman, come from two different worlds. The famous book *Men are from Mars, Women are from Venus* by John Gray, explains it well.

Here's a list of characteristics comparing the two brains:

MEN	WOMEN
Logical brain	Emotional brain
Speak 10,000 words/day	Speak 30,000 words/day
Driven by purpose & freedom	Driven by love & family
Link to universe	Link to mother earth
3 upper chakras	3 lower chakras
Men give advice & solution	Women want to be listened to
Men feel controlled	Women try to change us
When stressed, go to the nothing box (focused & withdrawn)	When stressed, need to talk (Overwhelmed & Emotionally involved)
Intimacy is like a rubber band	Intimacy is like a wave
Scoring points 1 to 10	Scoring points 1 to 1
Direct communication (what they think, straight to the point)	Indirect communication (Superlatives, Metaphors, Generalizations)
Grow by challenge	Grow by praise & support
Like direct criticism	Hurt & defensive by criticism
Straight honest	Testing her man all the time
Box for each thing	One box with everything all connected
Nothing box (fishing, zapping tv)	Can't do anything
Track record behavior	In the moment energy
Men don't understand body	Women have body temperature
More masculine energy needs	More feminine energy
Fix things by analyzing	Fix things with her surrender & love
Keeping our words	Words & facts take 2nd place after emotions and shifting moods

From this knowledge, choose one woman in your life you want to improve your relationship with. Then recall a confrontation with her and describe your new breakthrough understanding of why she acted and reacted like that. Finally, explain how you'll react next time with your new wisdom.

....

....

....

....

....

....

....

....

....

....

....

....

....

8.2. CRITERIA OF YOUR IDEAL LIFE PARTNER

🕐 5 minutes to complete

Whether you have a spouse or not, it is always useful to know what you need and look for in the person you're with. List all criteria of your dream life partner. It will help you see what you need to work on.

....

....

....

....

....

....

....

What are my deal breakers?

_____
_____
_____
_____
_____
_____
_____
_____
_____
_____

Who do I need to become to attract and/or keep this partner?

_____
_____
_____
_____
_____
_____
_____
_____
_____
_____
_____

Conclusion

Wow, you have done it !!!

Now it's time to jump and fail as much as possible toward becoming a superior man. It's the only way, consistency every day, never ever give up, be hopeful, keep the excitement flowing and always be grateful for the journey. Happiness is not when you'll succeed, but it's found inside you at every micro moment.

Thank you so much for doing this workbook, it means everything to us. We've put all our love and experiences here to hopefully make an impact. Our intention was to bring a more conscious man supporting the universe toward collective abundance. We hope you can share it with your friends and family and you can all push each other to your higher self.

Please don't forget to write an Amazon review, your support means everything.

JF Brou & Ivaylo Govedarov

Xoxo

If you need anything, don't hesitate. We are here for you.

But remember, all the answers are inside you. Meditate.

"WHAT THE SUPERIOR MAN SEEKS IS IN HIMSELF;
WHAT THE SMALL MAN SEEKS IS IN OTHERS"

~ CONFUCIUS

Appendix

1.) BOOKS WE BUILD THE WORKSHOP ON

King, Warrior, Magician, Lover: Rediscovering the Archetypes of the Mature Masculine
https://www.amazon.com/King-Warrior-Magician-Lover-Rediscovering/dp/0062506064/

The Way of the Superior Man: A Spiritual Guide to Mastering the Challenges of Women, Work, and Sexual Desire (20th Anniversary Edition)
https://www.amazon.com/Way-Superior-Man-Challenges-Anniversary-ebook/dp/B01NA993PI/

The Emotion Code: How to Release Your Trapped Emotions for Abundant Health, Love, and Happiness
https://www.amazon.com/Emotion-Code-Emotions-Abundant-Happiness/dp/1250214505/

Men Are from Mars, Women Are from Venus: Practical Guide for Improving Communication
https://www.amazon.com/Men-Mars-Women-Venus-Communication-ebook/dp/B00IHZ91T6/

Iron John: A Book about Men
https://www.amazon.com/Iron-John-Book-about-Men/dp/0306824264/ref=sr_1_1?keywords=iron+john&qid=1581360021&sr=8-1

The Enlightened Sex Manual: Sexual Skills for the Superior Lover
https://www.amazon.com/Enlightened-Sex-Manual-Sexual-Superior/dp/1591795850/ref=sr_1_1?keywords=enlightened+sex&qid=1581360053&sr=8-1

The Mask of Masculinity: How Men Can Embrace Vulnerability, Create Strong Relationships, and Live Their Fullest Lives
https://www.amazon.com/Mask-Masculinity-Embrace-Vulnerability-Relationships/dp/B076DKS6L6/

2.) MAN ARCHETYPES

The Divine Masculine (How To Awaken The Divine Masculine Within You) - Teal Swan
https://www.youtube.com/watch?v=p1Ahy6m4wHM

THE KING
What Makes a Great King? Exploring the Archetype of the King in Movies and Television
https://www.youtube.com/watch?v=1pOnHjRK7BU

THE MAGICIAN
Venturing into Sacred Space | Archetype of the Magician
https://www.youtube.com/watch?v=4unDD4OUUNQ

THE WARRIOR

The Archetype of the Warrior – How Films Help Empower Us All

https://www.youtube.com/watch?v=UlKuE7jm0WM

THE LOVER

The Lover Within | How Moonlight Relates to ALL Men

https://www.youtube.com/watch?v=NOis3-phW8Q

3.) SUPERIOR MAN FOUNDATION

The Way of The Superior Man by David Deida >> Animated Book Summary—How to Be a Man

https://www.youtube.com/watch?v=-5d4ea_q7mo

What Every Woman Should Know About Men

https://www.youtube.com/watch?v=Q3WsgZZtL50

10 Easy Habits That Make Men MORE ATTRACTIVE | Alex Costa

https://www.youtube.com/watch?v=yJYc-OntO24&

15 Signs You're An Alpha-Male

https://www.youtube.com/watch?v=AKLqZ6VnMG4

4.) EMOTIONS

Emotion Code - Process of Releasing Trapped Emotion

https://www.youtube.com/watch?v=N7S66OSNDil&

Emotions Definitions

http://www.themarriagelibrary.com/EmotionCode/Definition-of-Emotions.pdf

Emotional Chart

https://www.google.com/search?q=emotional+code+chart&safe=active&sxsrf=ACYBGNTfMNCfL0Mc-jWmqWtJ2SiXNyrjQFg:1580758571444&source=lnms&tbm=isch&sa=X&ved=2ahUKEwjao4HJkLbnA-hXRt1kKHZYlAaYQ_AUoAXoECA0QAw&biw=1366&bih=608#imgrc=wbGCX0ib_Kz22M

E-Motion Documentary www.e-motionthemovie.com

https://www.youtube.com/watch?v=FGRBuhllNnU

Heal Documentary

https://www.youtube.com/watch?v=s5Hpm-6Inxc

Bioenergetic Morning Rituals w/ Troy The Health Nut

https://www.youtube.com/watch?v=M9NhtLS1owM

How To Heal The Emotional Body - Teal Swan
https://www.youtube.com/watch?v=c3V_Gtfr_YA

5.) ENLIGHTEN SEXUALITY

My First Tantric Orgasm - (Male Orgasm Without Ejaculation)
https://www.youtube.com/watch?v=QeyD9OWKm1g

Introduction to Tantric Sex
https://www.youtube.com/watch?v=8zxZrUtUm5c

The Truth About Multiple Orgasms for Men - (It's not what you think...)
https://www.youtube.com/watch?v=yrV-T6qIthQ

MOST POWERFUL SEXUAL SUBLIMATION TECHNIQUE EVER !!!
https://www.youtube.com/watch?v=eqKnYqhJR0I

6.) MEN'S VS. WOMEN'S BRAIN

A Tale of Two Brains
https://www.youtube.com/watch?v=3XjUFYxSxDk

Men Are from Mars, Women Are from Venus: Practical Guide for Improving Communication
https://www.amazon.com/Men-Mars-Women-Venus-Communication-ebook/dp/B00IHZ91T6/

Mars brain, Venus brain: John Gray at TEDxBend
https://www.youtube.com/watch?v=xuM7ZS7nodk

Personal Notes:

Made in the USA
Middletown, DE
06 April 2023

28305794R00027